Revised and updated

Understanding People In The Past

The ANCIENT GREEKS

ROSEMARY REES

Heinemann Library
Chicago, Illinois

© 1997, 2006 Heinemann Library
a division of Reed Elsevier Inc.
Chicago, Illinois

Customer Service 888-454-2279
Visit our website at www.heinemannraintree.com

Designed by Michelle Lisseter and Damco Solutions Ltd
Printed in China

10 09 08 07 06
10 9 8 7 6 5 4 3 2 1

New edition ISBNs: 1 403 48747 2 (hardcover)
                    1 403 48753 7 (paperback)

The Library of Congress has cataloged the first edition as follows:
Rees, Rosemary, 1942-
    The ancient Greeks / Rosemary Rees.
        p. cm. -- (Understanding people in the past)
    Includes bibliographical references and index.
    Summary: Shows how the people of ancient Greece lived by describing their government, social customs, religion, and some aspects of their history.
    ISBN 0-431-07790-8 (lib. bdg.)   ISBN 1-58810-315-3 (pbk. bdg.)
    1.   Greece—Civilization—To 146 B.C.—Juvenile literature. [1. Greece—Civilization—To 146 B.C.]   I. Title. II. Series.
    DF77.R38   1997
    938—dc21
    96-53222 CIP AC

Acknowledgments
The author and publisher are grateful to the following for permission to reproduce copyright material:
a=above, b=below, c=center, l=left, r=right
Agora Excavation 1970, American School of Classical Studies at Athens p. 40b; Ancient Art and Architecture Collection pp. 7a and b. 11a and b, 16a, 17, 19b, 20a and b, 21c, 22, 27, 32a, 36, 37b, 46a and b, 56b; Bridgeman Art Library, p. 9, 58; C. M. Dixon, pp. 4a, 6, 8, 13a, 21a and b, 23, 31a, 32b, 45b, 50b; Ekdotike Athenon, pp. 2, 19a, 24, 25a, 34a, 49, 55a and b; Robert Harding Photographic Library, pp. 26, 38a, 43; Hirmer Fotoarchiv, p. 31; Michael Holford, pp. 4b, 10, 12, 13b, 15a and b; Kunsthistorisches Museum, Vienna, p. 56a; Mansell Collection, pp. 14, 16b, 38b; Metropolitan Museum of Art, New York, purchase 1947, Joseph Pulitzer Bequest, p. 40a; National Bibliothek Osterreichische, p. 25b; Picturepoint, p. 34b; Planet Earth Pictures, p. 45a (photograph Flip Schulke), Scala, p. 41a.

Cover photograph © The Art Archive / Museo Nazionale Taranto / Daglo Orti.

The publishers would like to thank Dr. Michael Vickers for his advice on the content of this book.

Some words are shown in bold, **like this**. You can find out what they mean by looking in the glossary.

CONTENTS

WHO WERE THE GREEKS?

People today still admire the work of Greek thinkers, writers, and artists who lived a very long time ago.

The Minoans

About 5,000 years ago people living on the island of Crete began to build and paint and make beautiful objects. They knew how to read and write, but their language was not Greek. They were called the Minoans because one of their kings was named King Minos.

This is a ruined Greek temple. There are lots of ruins like this. They are looked after now so that they do not collapse any further.

Greek craftsmen made beautiful jewelry like this. They used silver, gold, and precious stones. This jewelry was made thousands of years ago.

The first Greeks

The first Greek-speaking people moved onto mainland Greece about 2000 BC. They came from the north and the east. They learned from the Minoans and built beautiful palaces at places like Mycenae. Gradually, in each town and surrounding country areas, people began living in small groups. These towns were called **city-states.** By 450 BC Athens was one of the largest city-states. Greek learning and ideas spread far and wide.

This map shows the most important Greek city-states.

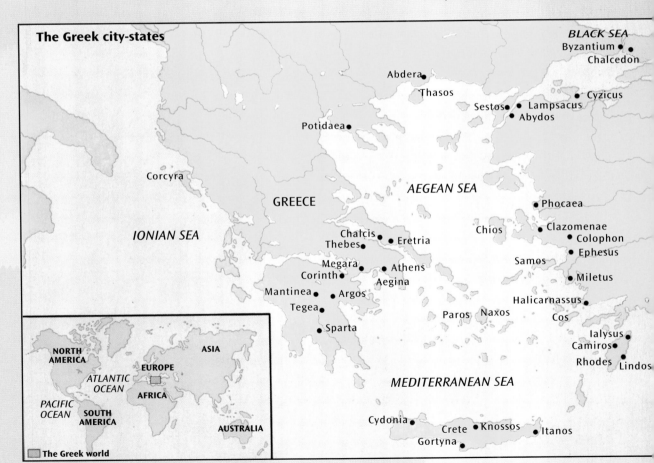

The Greek city-states

BLACK SEA
Byzantium
Chalcedon
Abdera
Thasos
Sestos Cyzicus
Lampsacus
Abydos
Potidaea

Corcyra

AEGEAN SEA

GREECE

Phocaea

Chios Clazomenae
Colophon
Ephesus

IONIAN SEA

Chalcis
Thebes Eretria
Samos

Megara
Corinth Athens
Aegina Miletus

Mantinea Argos
Tegea Halicarnassus

Paros Naxos
Cos

Sparta

MEDITERRANEAN SEA

Ialysus
Camiros
Rhodes Lindos

NORTH
AMERICA
ASIA

EUROPE
ATLANTIC
OCEAN
AFRICA
PACIFIC
OCEAN
SOUTH
AMERICA
AUSTRALIA

Cydonia
Knossos
Crete Itanos
Gortyna

The Greek world

5

HOW DO WE KNOW ABOUT THE GREEKS?

If you visited a museum you could look at objects or **artifacts** made and used by the Greeks. You could see artifacts such as coins and toys, statues and jewelry. Most of these artifacts were dug out of the ground by **archaeologists.** These are people who have been specially trained to **excavate** and uncover ruins of old buildings and towns. They also find every day objects, including pieces of pots and tiles. Using what they find, the archaeologists build a picture of the past.

Archaeologists at work. They are slowly uncovering evidence from the past.

Heinrich Schliemann found this gold cup at Mycenae. It was badly squashed. Archaeologists pushed it back into its correct shape.

Archaeologists have to decide where to look. They study what is already known about an area first. Sometimes they find clues in old books and maps. This is how they discovered the ruins of Mycenae. The city was destroyed 3,200 years ago, but people still told stories about the Mycenaeans. The Greek poet, Homer, wrote two long poems about them, called the *Iliad* and the *Odyssey*. A German businessman, Heinrich Schliemann, loved these poems. He decided to look for the lost cities they described. In 1870 he found the ruins of Troy and in 1876 he found Mycenae.

Archaeologists found this gold and silver dagger at Mycenae. The design is like the work of Minoan artists. Archaeologists think artists from Crete came to work in Mycenae.

CLUES IN WORDS AND PICTURES

Heinrich Schliemann decided where to look for Troy and Mycenae after reading Homer's poems. Archaeologists have found even older pieces of Greek writing, but not in books. In 1900 Arthur Evans began digging at Knossos. He found clay tablets with writing on them. There were two types of writing. These he called Linear A and Linear B.

The Greek alphabet			
Capital letter	**Small letter**	**Name**	**Sound**
A	α	alpha	a
B	β	beta	b
Γ	γ	gamma	g
Δ	δ	delta	d
E	ε	epsilon	e (as in *bed*)
Z	ζ	zeta	z
H	α	eta	a (as in *bay*)
Θ	θ	theta	th (as in *think*)
I	ι	iota	i
K	κ	kappa	k
Λ	λ	lambda	l
M	μ	mu	m
N	ν	nu	n
Ξ	ξ	xi	x
O	ο	omicron	o (as in *pot*)
Π	π	pi	p
P	ρ	rho	rh, r
Σ	σ	sigma	s
T	τ	tau	t
Υ	υ	upsilon	u
Φ	φ	phi	ph
X	χ	chi	kh
Ψ	ψ	psi	ps
Ω	ω	omega	o (as in *dome*)

Linear B
This clay tablet is about 3,400 years old. It is like the ones found by Arthur Evans. The writing on it is called Linear B. It took Michael Ventris 10 years to work out the language of Linear B. No one has yet worked out the older language, Linear A, used by the Minoans.

The alphabet we use today has many letters that come from ancient Greek letters. Can you work out which these are?

From about 700 BC many official records were carved on stone. These tell us about Greek laws and about how places were built. We can also learn a lot about Greek life from Homer and from other writers. Plato, a thinker and **philosopher,** wrote about his own ideas and those of his teacher, Socrates. Herodotus tried to separate the facts of the Greek past from stories that were told about it.

The Greeks put pictures of their daily life on jars, cups, vases, and bowls. Greek sculptures and paintings show us what the ancient Greeks wore and what they looked like.

Museums in London, Paris, and New York have many Greek objects that archaeologists found and took away with them.

The painting on this pot shows Greek farmers collecting olives. Two men use sticks to shake the fruit from the tree onto a sheet spread on the ground. A third man picks up the fruit. Olives are still picked in this way on Greek farms today.

The Greek civilizations			
3000 BC	The start of the Minoan civilization on Crete	1200 BC	Dorian invaders destroy the Mycenaean civilization
1600 BC	The Mycenaean civilization begins on the Greek mainland	1200–800 BC 800–475 BC 475–323 BC 323–30 BC	The Dark Ages The Archaic Period The Classical Period The Hellenistic Period

HOW GREECE WAS GOVERNED

Greece was a collection of independent city-states. Each state was ruled by a group of landowners who had as much power as a king. This is called an **aristocracy.** Sometimes an aristocracy was overthrown by a **tyrant.** Tyrants and nobles didn't obey any laws. By about 500 BC some of the city-states were ruled by **oligarchies.** In an oligarchy, the government is controlled by a few rich **citizens.** Gradually a new form of government was introduced in Athens. This was called **demokratia,** which means government by the people. The English word **democracy** comes from this Greek word. In Greek democracies, all citizens had a say in how their state was governed.

The Acropolis in Athens
The Acropolis was built as a fortress against invaders. Later it became a place of worship, with a temple to the city's special god.

How democracy worked in Athens

Each citizen of Athens was a member of the assembly. The assembly met once a week. Any citizen could speak at assembly meetings. A council of 500 citizens was chosen each year by drawing lots. The council decided what was to be discussed at assemblies. Council members looked after the management of the city. Each year a board of 10 generals was elected who were to be responsible for the protection of Athens against invaders.

Once a year, members of the assembly had the chance to throw out anyone they disliked. Each member scratched a name on a piece of pottery. These pieces were called ostraka. The person with the most votes against him was ostracized (sent away) for 10 years. This ostrakon shows the name of Aristeides.

Every year citizens of Athens took their turn at being judges, officials, and council members. The judges gave their verdicts on quarrels between citizens. They voted with bronze discs. If most of the discs used had solid knobs, the person was judged innocent. If most of the discs had hollow knobs, the person was guilty.

WHAT THE GREEKS WORE

In Greece the climate was dry with warm winters and very hot summers. People wore loose clothes to keep themselves cool. Men and women wore tunics called **chitons**. Men wore short tunics for work and long ones for special occasions. Workmen wore short brown tunics. Women wore chitons which came down to their ankles. Both men and women wore long, broad shawls called **himatia**. Men and women wore sandals or went barefoot.

This man is dressed for a special occasion. He is wearing a carefully arranged himation.

Hairstyles and makeup

Rich women folded their hair around headbands. Sometimes they bought wigs in the latest fashion. In Athens, men visited the beauty parlor as often as women did. They wanted to be fashionable, too. Men and women both wore perfume. Women used chalk to whiten their faces and juice to redden their lips.

Cloth and dyes

Most Greek clothes were made from wool. In Athens it was possible to buy a lighter cloth called linen, which was made from flax. Rich people could afford to buy brightly colored cloth for their clothes.

This woman is wearing a chiton. She has put a himation over it.

You can see various Greek hairstyles in this picture. All women except slaves had long hair. Some left it long and curly. Others tied or pinned it into fashionable styles.

FAMILY LIFE

Arranging a marriage

People felt it was their duty to get married and have children. Marriages were arranged by the fathers of the couple. The girl and boy did not have to love each other. Sometimes they did not meet until the wedding ceremony. All that mattered was that the wife-to-be would make a good mother. The girl's family arranged for her to give a **dowry**, which was usually a sum of money, to the young man she was to marry. Girls were usually married when they were about 15 years old. Boys were normally older.

This is a painting of a marriage procession. Only the very richest families could afford horses. Most brides rode to their new home in a cart pulled by mules or oxen. The bride sat with her bridegroom. Friends walked behind, carrying presents.

14

The wedding

Weddings were held at home. The bridegroom went to the bride's house. The bride's father gave her to the bridegroom. They rode in a chariot or cart to the groom's house. His family welcomed the new bride. They knelt by the fire and said prayers. The next day the bride's family visited them for a feast and brought presents.

A woman's life

Women spent most of their time at home. They spent their time weaving, cooking, and looking after the children. Women in richer families had servants and slaves to help them and do the cleaning and shopping. A husband could divorce his wife at any time, but he had to give back her dowry. He could also marry her off to someone else without her agreement. Wives could divorce their husbands, but they had to give reasons in writing.

How do we know?

Plutarch wrote about the lives of Greek leaders. Aristophanes and Menander wrote plays about ordinary people.

Archaeologists have found children's toys. They have found dolls, tops, and balls, and pictures of hoops and kites. They have found babies' feeding bottles like this one.

GOING TO SCHOOL

Children stayed at home until they were six or seven years old. They were looked after by their mothers. Richer families had servants to care for their children.

Teaching girls

Girls did not go to school. They learned to read, write, and count at home, and how to play a musical instrument. They learned to run a house, and they helped their mothers with household jobs.

Teaching boys

Most boys went to school when they were seven. They were taken by a slave called a **pedagogue.** Some parents could not afford to send their boys to school. These boys worked on the land instead.

This painting is on a pot. It shows a girl learning to read. She is reading from a scroll of papyrus. Scrolls are long sheets of paper, rolled up. Papyrus is Egyptian paper made from the papyrus reed.

Greek children learned to write on soft wax. The stylus scratched letters into the wax-coated surface of the writing tablet. Afterwards the wax could be smoothed over and the tablet was ready to use again.

16

The Greek philosophers

Greek philosophers had firm ideas about the way people should think and behave. They encouraged people to reason things out and to work out their own place in society.

The most famous Greek philosopher was Socrates. His pupil, Plato, and Plato's pupil Aristotle, left many writings about the philosophy of the Greeks.

Socrates, 469–399 BC

At school, boys learned to read, write, and count. They wrote with a pointed stick, called a **stylus,** on tablets coated with wax. They learned to count using beads on an **abacus.** When boys were 14 they went to a **palaistra,** which was a wrestling school. They learned wrestling, running, jumping, and throwing the javelin and discus. This was supposed to make them strong enough to fight.

Plato, 427–347 BC

Working

Many boys went to work with their fathers and grandfathers and learned a craft. These boys were **apprentices.** Some boys studied with a philosopher.

Aristotle, 384–322 BC

LIVING IN SPARTA

Life in Sparta was very different from life in the other Greek city-states. In Sparta, the only important thing was to be a brave soldier.

Children

Children belonged to the state. If babies were weak or ill when they were born, they were left to die. Children stayed at home with their mothers until they were seven. Then the boys were sent to boarding school. They learned to read and write, and were taught about hardship, hunger, and pain.

This is a bronze statue of a Spartan warrior. It was made about 500 BC.

This map shows Sparta and the rest of Greece.

The city of Sparta was built on a plain. You can see in this modern photograph that it was surrounded by mountains. These protected Sparta from invaders.

Life after school

All boys had to become soldiers when they left school. Their training made them the best soldiers in Greece. However, their life was very hard. They had to give all their time to the city-state. They could marry, but were not allowed to live with their wives until they were 30 years old.

The government of Sparta

The Spartan government was an oligarchy. This meant that a few people made the important decisions. These were the 30 members of the Council of Elders. The Spartans had two kings. One king led the army and the other king was the chief priest.

This is a statue of a girl from Sparta. Spartan women learned to jump, run, wrestle, and throw the discus and javelin. Spartans wanted strong mothers for their sons. Spartan girls wore short, sleeveless tunics. Other Greeks were shocked. They thought women's clothes should cover more of their bodies.

THE GODS OF OLYMPUS

The Greeks believed in many gods. They had many different ideas about the gods. Homer wrote about gods who looked and behaved like humans. Hesiod explained how the god Zeus used thunder and lightning to control rival gods. Xenophanes, a philosopher, thought there was only one god, while Protagoras was not sure that gods existed at all!

Greek people said that the 12 most important gods lived on Mount Olympus in northeast Greece. The Greeks told stories or **myths** about these gods.

This silver coin was made in Athens in about 470 BC. The owl was the symbol of the goddess Athena. The people of Athens believed Athena would protect their city of Athens.

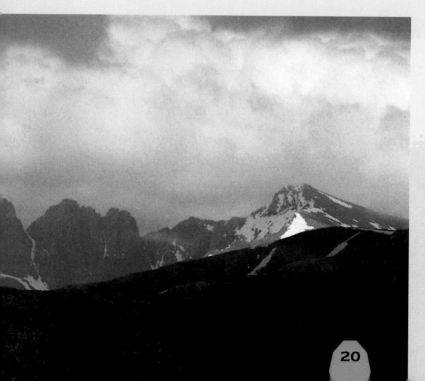

A modern photograph of Mount Olympus
The ancient Greeks thought this was where the gods lived.

The 12 Olympian gods

Zeus: the chief of the gods. God of the sky, storms, thunder, and lightning.

Hera: the wife of Zeus. Goddess of marriage and childbirth.

Poseidon: Zeus's brother and god of the sea. He used his trident to cause rough seas and earthquakes.

Demeter: goddess of farming and crops from the earth, especially grain. She was sister of Zeus and Poseidon.

Apollo: the god of light, thought, poetry, and music. He was a son of Zeus and Leto. People thought Apollo could tell them about the future.

Artemis: Apollo's twin sister, and the goddess of hunting and wild animals.

Ares: Zeus and Hera's son, the god of war.

Aphrodite: the goddess of love and beauty. No one knew who her parents were.

Hermes: the son of Zeus and Maia. He was the messenger of the gods who took the souls of dead people to the Underworld, a place with no sun in the center of the Earth.

Hephaistos: Zeus and Hera's crippled son. As the blacksmith god, he made thrones for all the gods and goddesses and armor for heroes.

Athena: the goddess of wisdom and war. She protected cities and arts and crafts. Athena taught Hephaistos how to use his tools.

Hestia: the goddess of the hearth and home. She was Zeus's sister and hated quarrels. One day Zeus announced that his son...

Dionysos, the god of wine, must have a seat on Olympus. Hestia gave up her place so there would not be an unlucky number of 13 gods and goddesses.

Apollo, the god of music, holding a lyre

Artemis, the goddess of hunting

Athena, the goddess of war, with her helmet and spear

TEMPLES AND SHRINES

The Greeks spoke to their gods with prayers, gifts, songs, and festivals. People prayed to the god whom they thought could help them most.

The Greeks had many gods and goddesses. They built temples for their gods and goddesses. Inside each temple there was a **shrine** with a statue of the god who was prayed to in it.

People believed that the gods liked rich and sparkling gifts. This golden bowl is decorated with a pattern of acorns and beechnuts.

The temple roof rested on walls and pillars.

Outer walls of the temple grounds, or *temenos.*

The inner part, or *cella.*

Statue of a god and a small table for offerings.

Outdoor altar.

A Greek temple

Offerings to the gods

People left gifts in front of the shrine. Then they prayed at the outdoor altar. If they wanted a special favor, like a good harvest, they killed an animal as an offering. They also made offerings if they thought the gods were angry.

Oracles

People went to an **oracle** for advice. This was a shrine where the priest or priestess had special powers. People wrote questions for the god on lead tablets. The god replied through the voice of the priest or priestess.

This is a photograph of the ruined temple of Apollo at Delphi. It was built in about 500 BC. The most famous oracle in all Greece was at Delphi. The Greek writers Aeschylus, Pindar, and Euripides all describe the temple. This helped the archaeologists to know what they had found when they dug it up.

MEDICINE AND HEALING

Asclepius, the god of healing

When people were ill, they visited one of the temples of
Asclepius. The priests of Asclepius tried to cure sick people.
The treatments they used were a mixture of bathing, rest,
fasting, simple foods, herbs, and magic. People who got well
again had their names and details of their cure carved on
stone blocks in the temples.

Hippocrates

Hippocrates changed the Greeks' ideas about medicine. He said
that patients should be examined to find out what was wrong.
Then the doctor should decide how to treat the illness.

This stone picture was
made as thanks for a cure.
It shows what happened
to the sick man. He went
to sleep in a temple
of Asclepius. He had a
dream. In the dream
Asclepius told him what
should be done to make
him better. When he woke
up the man told the priest
about his dream. Then the
priest knew what to do,
and the man was cured.

Greek surgery

Herophilus started a school of medicine in the Greek city of Alexandria. He was one of the first people to study dead bodies for science. He wrote about what he saw. This helped him teach Greek doctors about surgery.

People who were ill could go to Greek hospitals for free treatment. They had to pay if a doctor visited them at home!

This is a picture carved in stone. The man is offering a huge model of a leg as thanks for a cure to his leg. Archaeologists have found a lot of carvings like this.

This is a drawing from a book written by a Greek doctor 2,000 years ago. It is a picture of a herb he used to make his patients better. People have used herbs to cure illnesses for thousands of years. They are still used today.

FARMS AND FARMERS

Farming in Greece was not easy. The weather is hot and dry. There are mountains with thin soil. In the valleys, however, the soil is good. Farmers had to choose their crops carefully. They grew wheat, barley, fruit, and vegetables in the valleys. Herds of goats and sheep grazed on the mountainsides. Grape vines and olive trees grew well in the poor soil.

The Greek farmers of today have the same problems as the farmers in ancient Greece. In this modern photograph you can see a hillside with thin soil in which crops will not grow. The farmer is grazing sheep on the land.

The Greek months

Gamelion	January–February
Anthesterion	February–March
Elaphebolion	March–April
Munychion	April–May
Thargelion	May–June
Skirophorion	June–July
Hecatombaion	July–August
Metageitnion	August–September
Boedromion	September–October
Pyanopsion	October–November
Maimacterion	November–December
Poseideon	December–January

Rich farmers employed **tenant farmers** to work the land for them. The tenant farmers had slaves to work for them. So did farmers who owned small farms. If there was a bad harvest, some farmers could not carry on. They became slaves.

The Greeks made pictures of everyday life to decorate their walls and floors. This is a tiled floor. It shows a man plowing.

THE GREEK CITY

The old cities of ancient Greece had narrow streets that twisted and turned. The buildings were crowded together. They were not planned. People added streets, houses, markets, and temples when they were needed. From about 500 BC the Greeks began to rebuild their cities. They built streets in straight lines which crossed each other at right angles. Buildings were put up in neat, straight lines.

*This is a photograph of a **stoa**, which is a covered way. The Greeks built them around their market places. This stoa is in Athens. It has been rebuilt by archaeologists.*

Acropolis

temples

gymnasium

stoa

agora

theater

stadium

This is a drawing of the city of Priene. Priene was built by the Greeks. You can see how they built straight streets and planned where the buildings should go. Priene was uncovered by archaeologists.

Doric style

Ionic style

Corinthian style

The Greeks used stone columns for most of their public buildings and temples. There were three main types of columns. Doric columns were the simplest, Ionic were more elaborate, and Corinthian were the most decorative of all.

Town planners designed the new cities. Hippodamus of Miletus was a town planner. He planned the rebuilding of Pireus, the port for Athens, in 450 BC.

After 700 BC the Greeks began to use stone instead of wood for their public buildings. They cut blocks of marble or limestone from their quarries. Then they carved the stone into shape. Columns were made by standing one block of stone on top of another. The blocks were held together by wooden pegs. In this photograph you can see, in the front, stone blocks that were used to make columns like those in the background.

A GREEK HOME

Archaeologists found about 100 houses at Olynthos, in north Greece. The houses once belonged to quite rich people. They left the city after a great battle in 348 BC. No one has lived there since.

dining room

women's rooms

bedrooms

store room

Kitchen

portico or front door

altar

courtyard

bathroom

slaves' room

dining room

store room   kitchen

courtyard

portico or
front door   altar

slaves' room

bathroom

The house of a rich Greek family in Olynthos probably looked like this. The rooms were built around a central courtyard. The women had their own rooms. There was a separate room for the slaves. The dining room was for the men.

Building a house

The Greeks built their fine public buildings from stone. They built their homes from mud bricks that they dried in the sun. These bricks were cheap and easy to make, but they crumbled after some years.

Furniture and decoration

Archaeologists find many artifacts in the houses they excavate. These tell us what the houses looked like and what people did in the different rooms. Some houses at Olynthos had patterned **mosaic** floors. The rooms were lit with small olive oil lamps. They were heated with pans of hot charcoal. Some houses had baths.

This stone carving shows that the Greeks kept clothes and blankets in wooden chests. Can you see a basket, a mirror, an oil jug, a cup, and a chair?

This wall painting shows men at a feast. They are lying on couches and have low tables in front of them. They are holding drinking bowls in their hands.

FOOD AND FUN

Cooking and eating

In many homes, work in the kitchen was done by slaves. They ground wheat or barley to make flour. They cooked food over an open fire or in an oven made from pottery. Some ovens could be taken outside. This kept the kitchen free of smoke.

The Greeks ate a lot of fish. They dried some of the fish to eat when the weather was bad and fishing was impossible. Farmers grew their own food and sold some of it to the cities. They made goats' milk cheese and ate eggs, vegetables, and lots of figs. Many families kept bees, and used the honey to sweeten their food. They made wine, and they crushed olives to make cooking oil.

The main meal was in the evening. The Greeks often invited guests to share their food. Women only ate dinner with the men if there was a party. From about 500 BC people began to eat more complicated meals. These took longer to prepare and cook. Rich families had a cook. They hired several cooks if there was going to be a feast.

This slave is collecting water from a fountain. All the water needed for cooking and washing had to be collected like this.

Archaeologists found this pottery model in a tomb. It shows a woman cooking over an open fire. She is using a fan to keep the oven at the right temperature.

Music and dancing

A feast was followed by entertainment. Sometimes there was a **symposium**, at which guests would speak on a particular subject. Xenophon, a Greek writer, wrote about a symposium where there were musicians, a dancer, and a **jester.** Greek musicians played two types of stringed instruments—the **lyre** and the **cithara.** They also played pipes called **auloi.** Very few pieces of written music have been found. We can only guess how Greek music sounded.

This is a painting on a wine jar. It was made about 440 BC. The woman in the middle is playing a kind of harp. Above her is a cithara. On the right, a young man is holding a lyre. On the left, a woman holds a pair of auloi.

The Greeks used music in many different ways. They had happy songs to celebrate the birth of a child. They had sad songs for death. There were working songs and love songs. There was dancing for happy and sad events.

THE THEATER

Every large city in Greece had a theater. Greek actors performed plays in huge open-air theaters. People crowded in to watch. Important citizens, such as priests and judges, had the best seats. The audience stayed all day and watched several plays. They took food with them to eat during the intermissions. It cost two **obols** to get in, but poor people got the money from the city-state. The plays were all about Greek gods and heroes. Everyone knew the stories. They enjoyed seeing how different writers told them. There were prizes for the best plays.

The theaters were so large that the audience could not see the actors' faces. They wore large masks to show the sort of person they were pretending to be. This is a mask from a statue of an actor.

This is the open-air theater at Epidauros. It is still used every summer. People today can sit on the same seats and see the same plays as Greek people saw 2,300 years ago.

Plays

All Greek actors were men. Women were not allowed to act in plays. There were three types of plays. Tragedies were about sad and solemn subjects. Comedies made people laugh. **Satyr plays** made fun of something serious. The most famous writers of tragedies were Aeschylus, Sophocles, and Euripides. They wrote more than 300 plays but only 33 have survived. The best known comedy writer was Aristophanes. Eleven of his plays have survived. Plays written by these men are still performed today.

The architect Polykleitos designed the theater at Epidauros in about 350 BC. This is a modern drawing of a similar theater. There was room for 14,000 people to watch plays. The chorus danced and sang in the area called the **orchestra**. *Behind that was the stage on which the actors performed. At the back of the stage was the* **skene**, *which was a permanent background made from stone.*

skene

stage

orchestra

THE GAMES

Acting and drama began as a way of praising the gods. Athletic competitions began in the same way. The Greeks held contests of strength at festivals for the gods. Gradually these developed into organized games. They held competitions in running, jumping, throwing the discus and javelin, wrestling, riding, and chariot racing. The Greeks held these competitions at different festivals. The Isthmian Games at Corinth were in honor of the sea-god Poseidon; the Pythian Games at Delphi were in honor of Apollo; and the Nemean Games at Nemea, and the Olympic Games at Olympia were in honor of the god Zeus.

Between 1958 and 1962 archaeologists excavated the stadium at Olympia. It is about 197 yards long.

This pot painting shows different athletic events. Athletes were usually naked. There were wrestling and boxing competitions, discus and javelin throwing, running, and the long jump where men had to hold weights as they jumped. Can you see the man jumping with weights in the picture?

The Olympic Games

These Games were held every four years. Messengers went to all parts of Greece to announce the date. The Games began with a sacrifice to Zeus.

The athletes were not professionals. They were ordinary men and boys who had trained long and hard and were very fit. Any men except slaves and foreigners could take part. There were even events for children. Women, however, could only watch. The winners were given garlands of olive leaves. Their prize was the glory of winning.

The Greeks loved to watch horse racing. The main event at the Olympic Games was the chariot race. Prizes went to the owners of the horses and the chariots, not to the drivers.

WORK AND WORKMEN

Most Greeks worked as farmers. In the cities, however, people had other jobs. The Greeks did not like to work for a master. They preferred to work for themselves because it made them more independent.

Craftsmen

Craftsmen set up their own workshops to make things the townspeople needed. Carpenters made wooden furniture. Smiths used metals such as iron and bronze to make knives and armor. Basket makers used reeds to make baskets. These were used for storing wool, fruit, and grain. Silversmiths and potters made cups, plates, bowls, and jars. All craftspeople were men. Women worked at home.

In this picture a cobbler is making a sandal. Tools for shaping and sewing shoes hang on the wall ready for him to use.

In this picture the customer is standing ready for the cobbler to draw around her feet. This is so that he can get the right shape and make sure her sandals will fit.

Slaves

Some Greeks did not have to work at all because they owned slaves. Slaves were always foreigners. They were often people who had been captured during a war and brought back to Greece. Rich families had many slaves. Even the poorer farmers had slaves to help them. Slaves had no freedom. They had to do everything their master wanted. This gave Greek men the time to go to assembly meetings and take part in the government of the city-state.

This pot painting shows workers heating metals in a furnace. Metal-workers made knives and cooking pots. Men who worked with bronze made buckles and helmets for the army. Silver and gold-workers made jewelry and vases.

THE AGORA

The **agora** was a large open space in the center of most Greek cities. The word agora meant a meeting or assembly. Later it came to mean a marketplace.

The marketplace

The Greeks divided the agora into areas for different types of produce. The areas were called "fish," "wine," "cheese" and so on. The market traders put out their goods on stalls to sell. Bankers sat at counters on the agora. They were ready to lend money to people who wanted to borrow. Markets were always very busy.

The men on this painted pot are weighing goods. They are using balance scales. Greek weights were called talents. One talent was nearly 58 pounds.

This is a model of the agora in Athens. It shows what it might have looked like. Model makers get their information from archaeologists.

On two sides of the agora there were workshops for silversmiths, bronze workers, and stone carvers. These craftsworkers got plenty of customers because the market was busy. On the other two sides of the agora there were temples, law courts, and the building where the assembly met. At the edge of the agora, groups of slaves waited to be hired for work or bought by new owners.

This vase painting shows a fish seller. He is using a large knife to cut pieces of fish for a customer.

Greek coins

At first the Greeks traded by swapping goods. They did not use money until 900 BC. Then they used thin rods of iron called **obeloi.** A bundle of obeloi was called a **drachma.** By about 550 BC each city-state had its own coins. Most coins were made of silver because there was not much gold in Greece. Archaeologists have found thousands of Greek coins. Some of the pictures on them tell us what the Greeks thought their gods looked like. This coin from Dodona shows the head of Zeus.

COLONIES AND TRADE

Colonies

Between 750 BC and 650 BC there were so many people in Greece that there was not enough land to grow food for everyone. The city-states sent people to find other land to farm. These people settled near the sea. They planted grain and vegetables to grow food. They built new city-states. They had to be independent. They could not rely on the city-states back home. As these **colonies** became more organized, the people began to trade.

This map shows where the Greeks set up colonies. They had colonies in Italy, Sicily, North Africa, and Asia Minor. The map also shows the goods they traded.

BRITAIN

SCYTHIA
timber
slaves

Olbia■

Dioscurias■

SPAIN

■ Massalia

ITALY
meat copper
wool linen

Odessus

THRACE
iron copper
grain slaves

■ Sinope
iron fish nuts

■ Heraclea

■ Neapolis

MACEDONIA
timber gold
silver

ASIA MINOR

Sybaris■

Phoecaea

■ Croton

Corinth■ ■Athens
oil wine

■ Miletus

Phaselis

■ Al Mina

Selinus■

Sparta■

silver pottery
metalwork

■ Rhodes

Salamis

Sicily
grain
timber

■ Syracuse

Cyprus
grain oil
timber
copper

CARTHAGE
rugs cushions

Crete

MEDITERRANEAN SEA

SYRIA
slaves
dates
dyes

NORTH AFRICA

■ Cyrene
wool grain
silphium, a vegetable

■ Naucratis

EGYPT
grain papyrus
flax ivory

Key
● cities of the Greek homeland
■ Greek colonies

Trade

If people living in the colonies had more goods than they needed, they sent them to Greece. They sent grain, timber, and metals. They bought goods they needed, such as pottery, oil, silver, wool, and papyrus.

Athens had a large fleet of trading ships. Each trader had his own ship. Traders sailed from April to September when the weather was good. They bought and sold at different ports. They traded with Greek colonies. They traded with other countries around the Mediterranean Sea, including Syria, northern Italy and Egypt. Many of the traders were foreigners who were not allowed to own land in Greece.

Ships carried goods and people between the islands, the mainland, and other countries. The quickest way to travel was by sea.

TRAVEL

The easiest way to travel was by ship. Ships kept as close to land as possible. When they had to sail across the open sea, Greek sailors steered using the sun during the day and the stars at night. The Greeks had big wooden ships to carry goods. These **merchant ships** carried cargo to countries around the Mediterranean Sea. They were slow, and were often attacked by pirates. The Greeks guarded their cargo ships with warships called **triremes.**

This painted bowl was made in Athens in about 500 BC. It shows a heavy, wide merchant ship on the left and a long, narrow trireme on the right. Paintings like this show archaeologists what ancient ships looked like. Then they can put together the remains they find.

A Trireme

linen sails

A bronze spike to ram enemy ships.

Foot soldiers, archers, and officers stood on the deck to ward off pirates and invaders.

Long oars at the stern help to steer the ship.

bow

A painted eye to keep off evil spirits and to help the ship "see" its way.

The hull was made of fir which was lighter than oak.

The keel was made of oak which was heavy but strong.

Three rows of oars meant more rowers could fit into a small space. The bottom rows of oars came through portholes.

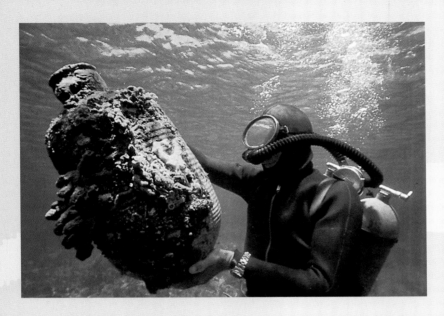

Archaeologists work underwater as well as on land. This archaeologist is looking at an amphora. An amphora is a large pottery storage jar. They were used on ships to carry goods such as oil, grain, and wine.

When people had to travel by land, they walked or they rode on horseback. Sometimes they used carts which were pulled by horses. The carts carried passengers and luggage. Goods were carried in carts, too, or in baskets on the backs of donkeys. Rich people might ride in chariots.

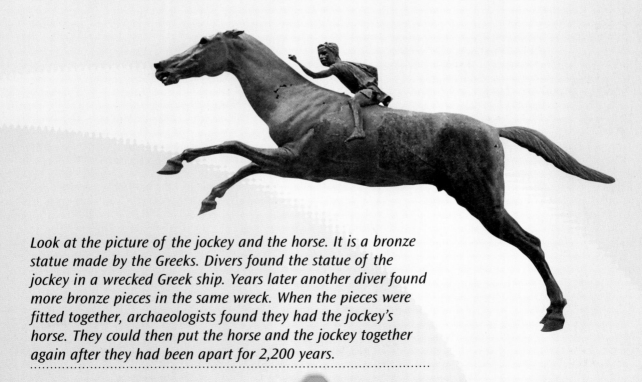

Look at the picture of the jockey and the horse. It is a bronze statue made by the Greeks. Divers found the statue of the jockey in a wrecked Greek ship. Years later another diver found more bronze pieces in the same wreck. When the pieces were fitted together, archaeologists found they had the jockey's horse. They could then put the horse and the jockey together again after they had been apart for 2,200 years.

GREEK SOLDIERS

Each city-state had its own army. Young men trained as soldiers for two years when they left school. Then they were called up to join the army if there was a war. Only Sparta had a full-time army.

Hoplites

Ordinary foot soldiers, called **hoplites,** had to buy their own armor and weapons. A hoplite had to buy his own helmet, shield, sword, breastplate, spear, and leg protectors. If a man could not afford to do this, he had to become an oarsman on a trireme.

This is a Greek helmet of a kind made in Corinth. Each region had a different shaped helmet.

The painting on this pot shows a hoplite in armor. He is wearing a short, pleated tunic and a helmet. He is carrying a shield and a spear. This hoplite has bare feet, but other paintings show them wearing sandals.

The first five rows of hoplites held their spears out in front of them. The spears were very long. The hoplites could hit their enemies without having to get too close. Row after row of hoplites marched toward enemy soldiers like a battering ram.

Phalanx fighting

When the hoplites fought they stood very close together so that each man's body was partly protected by his neighbor's shield. When they fought, 256 hoplites made a great square shape called a **phalanx.** Slowly the phalanx moved forward and forced the enemy soldiers apart. Then the **cavalry** moved in and forced the enemy to run away.

Greek armor

We know a lot about Greek armor. This is because it was made from metal. Metal lasts a long time. Hoplites wore bronze helmets and breastplates. They had bronze shields called hopla. Their leg protectors were made from bronze. Each hoplite carried a sword which was about 28 inches long and a spear which was 6 to 10 feet long. The army from Thebes had spears which were 20 feet long.

WAR ON LAND AND AT SEA

City-states such as Athens and Sparta were great rivals and often fought each other. However, when a foreign army threatened Greece, the city-states asked each other for help.

The Battle of Marathon

In 490 BC King Darius of Persia sent an army to attack Athens. He wanted revenge. Eight years earlier the Athenians had burned the important Persian city of Sardis.

King Cyrus the Great made Persia the biggest empire in the world. He ruled over his empire from palaces at Babylon, Persepolis, and Susa. Some city-states, including those of Ionia, were part of his empire.

EUROPE

THRACE

BLACK SEA

CASPIAN SEA

Thermopylae

Hellespont

Salamis

Marathon   LYDIA

Plataea

Athens   Sardis

Sparta

IONIA

ASIA

MEDITERRANEAN SEA

Babylon

Susa

Jerusalem

Persepolis

THE GULF

The Persian Empire in 500 BC
Key
X   main battles
     Persian empire

48

The Athenian army, led by general Miltiades, defeated the strong Persian force at the Battle of Marathon. A messenger ran 26 miles from Marathon to Athens with the news.

Thermopylae

Darius' son, Xerxes, was determined to defeat the Greeks. In 480 BC he led a huge army into Greece. The Spartans joined the war on the side of the Athenians. The Greeks fought bravely, but they were defeated by the Persians at Thermopylae. The Persians marched on toward Athens.

The Battle of Salamis

Themistocles, the Athenian commander, ordered everyone to leave Athens. The women and children went to the islands. The men joined the triremes to fight at sea. Themistocles tricked the Persian fleet so that they sailed into a narrow channel between Greece and the island of Salamis. Greek triremes were waiting for them. The Persians lost most of their ships in the battle.

This sculpture is supposed to be of Themistocles. It was made by a Roman but he copied it from a Greek sculpture which has been lost.

THE ATHENIAN EMPIRE

The Athenian navy defeated the Persians at Salamis in 480 BC. The Spartan army defeated the Persians at the Battle of Platea in 479 BC. Nevertheless the Greeks were still afraid of attacks by the Persians.

The Delian League

The Athenians said that the Greek city-states should join together in a **league.** More than 200 city-states and islands joined. It was called the Delian League because its headquarters was on the island of Delos. The city-states and islands built up the Athenian navy. They defeated the Persians in 466 BC.

Pericles was leader of Athens between 448 BC and 429 BC. He planned wonderful new buildings to make Athens the most beautiful city in the world.

This is the Parthenon in Athens. The Persians had destroyed the buildings on the Acropolis hill. The Greeks built the Parthenon to thank the gods for saving the people of Athens from the Persians.

Athens protected the other city-states. They paid for this protection. Athens became more powerful. The league became an Athenian empire. Eventually the Athenians made all the league members use Athenian coins.

The people of Athens now had money to spend on statues, paintings, and beautiful buildings. They had time to read and write and discuss ideas.

The Parthenon
The sculptor Pheidias made a statue of Athena from gold and ivory that stood more than 30 feet (9 meters) high. It disappeared long ago. Pheidias was in charge of the craftspeople who carved marble statues and scenes of Athenian life for the Parthenon. All the carvings were once brightly painted. The carvings in the picture are part of the marble frieze at the top of the temple.

THE PELOPONNESIAN WAR

Many Athenians dreamed of the day when Greece would be one state with Athens as the capital. The Athenian navy began to attack some city-states to force them to join the Athenian Empire. The smaller city-states asked Sparta to help them. Sparta and other city-states joined together in the Peloponnesian League. In 431 BC they declared war on Athens.

This map shows how power was divided in the war. Sparta controlled the area called the Peloponnese in the south. Athens had supporters on the islands and in western Asia Minor.

Key
- ○ cities which supported Athens
- ● cities which supported Sparta
- ✕ main battles won by Athens
- ✗ main battles won by Sparta

Lysander and Alcibiades

Alcibiades lived in Athens. He was rich and famous. He hoped that the war would bring him more power. It was his idea to attack Sicily. Sadly for him, this was where the Athenian fleet lost their first battle. It was Lysander, the Spartan admiral, who finally defeated the Athenian fleet.

This statue is of Thucydides. He wrote a history of the Peloponnesian War.

The Spartans and Athenians fought battle after battle. The Spartans could not capture Athens. The city walls were too strong. The Athenian navy attacked Sparta's allies from the sea. The Peloponnesian League did not have enough ships to defeat Athens' navy. Then the Spartans decided to get help from the Persians. The Persians gave them enough money to build a fleet of ships. A Spartan general, Lysander, launched a surprise attack in the harbor at Aegospotami. He defeated the Athenian fleet there. Then he sailed back to Piraeus, the port for Athens. His ships stopped food from getting into Athens. People starved and Athens was forced to surrender.

This shows a wife saying good-bye to her husband who is going to war.

THE DEFEAT OF THE CITY-STATES

Sparta defeated Athens in the Peloponnesian War. At first the Greek city-states were glad to be free from the rule of the Athenian Empire. However, they soon realized that they were worse off than before. The Spartans tried to rule the city-states themselves. They were harsh rulers.

Philip of Macedon made Pella his capital city. He took over the gold and silver mines of his neighbors. He trained his men to be fierce soldiers and horsemen.

MACEDONIA

THRACE

Pella •

Vergina •

GREECE

AEGEAN SEA

Chaeronea ✗   • Thebes

• Athens

Key
O gold and silver mines

Sparta •

General Epaminondas of Thebes

Fighting broke out between the city-states and Sparta. General Epaminondas of the city-state of Thebes tried out a new idea. His soldiers fought in a crescent shape. When the Spartans attacked, the Theban soldiers moved to surround them. In this way the Thebans put an end to Spartan rule.

Philip of Macedon

Macedonia was a wild mountainous area in the north of Greece. The people there were ruled by a king. In 359 BC Philip II was king of Macedonia. He wanted to rule over all of Greece. In 338 BC Philip's huge army defeated the Greeks at a place called Chaeronea. The Greeks had to accept Philip as their leader.

Archaeologists discovered the royal tombs of Philip and his family. They were at a place called Vergina. This head is made from ivory. It is of Philip of Macedon.

This tomb at Vergina was full of rich treasures. The archaeologists found a gold crown, a gold arrow quiver, silver cups and bowls, and bronze armor. The tomb is decorated with pictures of a lion hunt.

ALEXANDER THE GREAT

Alexander was a brave and brilliant leader. He loved Greek poetry and art, and was interested in science. Just like his father, Philip of Macedon, he wanted to conquer other lands.

First, Alexander united all the city-states of Greece. Then he turned to attack Greece's old enemy, Persia. He defeated the King of Persia, Darius III. All the lands of Persia came under the Greek rule of Alexander. Alexander treated the Persians carefully. They had once been rulers of his empire. They could revolt at any time and defeat his empire. He said that his men should marry Persian women. He set an example by marrying Roxane from Sogdiana. She was Persian.

Alexander was only 32 when he died from a fever in 323 BC. He made no plans for his empire after his death. Eventually three of his generals took parts of his empire. They ruled over them as kings.

This is a picture of Alexander and Olympias, his mother.

This is a temple at Petra in Jordan. It looks Greek, because of the influence of Alexander who ruled over Jordan as part of his empire.

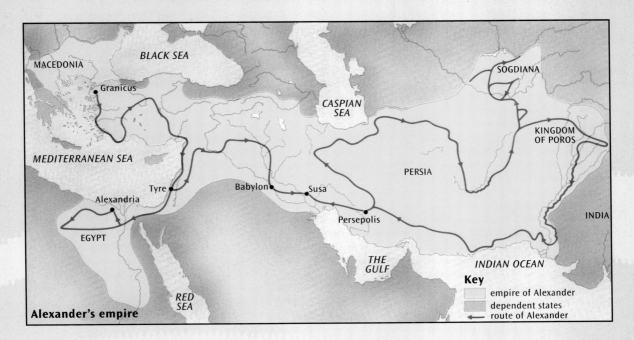

MACEDONIA
BLACK SEA
Granicus
SOGDIANA
CASPIAN
SEA
KINGDOM
OF POROS
MEDITERRANEAN SEA
PERSIA
Tyre
Babylon
Susa
INDIA
Alexandria
Persepolis
EGYPT
THE
GULF
INDIAN OCEAN
RED
SEA
Key
empire of Alexander
dependent states
route of Alexander
Alexander's empire

*This is a map of Alexander's empire.
Alexander and his army fought for 11
years to gain this empire. The red line
shows where he and his army went.*

Science in Greece 323–330 BC

Many famous discoveries were made in the Greek Empire at
this time.

Euclid and Pythagoras worked out the rules of geometry.

Aristarchus found out that the sun, not the earth, is the center
of our universe.

Eratosthenes worked out the distance around the earth.

Ptolemy I set up a special institute for research at Alexandria
in Egypt. It was called the Mouseion. It was a place where
poets, scientists, and scholars could study.

THE RISE OF ROME

The Romans built a trading center on the Tiber River in Italy. This grew into the city of Rome. The Romans began to trade with the cities around the Mediterranean Sea. They wanted power. In 146 BC they conquered Carthage in North Africa. Then they turned their attention to Greece.

The Romans gradually took over Alexander's empire. In 168 BC a Roman army destroyed Macedonia. Then the Roman general, Pompey, defeated the King of Syria in 65 BC. The Roman Emperor Augustus took over Egypt in 30 BC. The Romans had become the most powerful rulers in the world.

This is a painting of philosophers in ancient Greece. It was painted in Renaissance times. It shows what the painter Raphael imagined the philosophers to have been like.

The legacy of Greece

The Romans were fascinated by Greek art, architecture, and learning. They took Greek works of art to Rome. They copied Greek architecture. Young Romans went to Athens to learn from the philosophers and artists. Invaders conquered Rome in AD 476. People forgot about Greek and Roman art and learning. Nearly 1,000 years later some people in Italy began to read Greek philosophy. They paid archaeologists to look for Greek statues and paintings. This was the beginning of the **Renaissance.** Ancient Greek civilization has influenced people ever since.

This pot was made in about 1790. It was made at a factory in England, which belonged to Josiah Wedgwood. You can see that it is very like the pots made in ancient Greece but it is more delicate.

This is the British Museum in London. It was built between 1823 and 1847. It has Ionic columns and carved decorations which are like those in ancient Greece.

TIME LINE

BC

c 2000   First Greek-speaking peoples invade Greek mainland. Minoan civilization begins on Crete.

1600   Mycenaean civilization of Greece begins. Small, rich kingdoms flourish.

1200   The kingdoms of the Mycenaeans are threatened by the Dorians from the north.

1150   The Mycenaean kingdoms are destroyed. The Mycenaean Age ends and the Dark Ages begin.

850–600   Homer writes his epic poems, the *Iliad* and the *Odyssey*.
The Greeks adopt a new alphabet. Some people begin to leave their Greek homeland and set up colonies in the land around the Mediterranean Sea. The Dark Ages end and the Archaic Period begins.

776   First Olympic Games held.

600–475   During the Archaic Period many city-states are governed by oligarchies. Greek coins are first made. By the end of this period democracy begins in Athens.

546   The Persians conquer Ionia as their empire spreads.

500   Archaic Period ends. Classical Period begins.

493   Ionian and Athenian supporters try to rebel against Persian rule, but are defeated.

490   Persians invade Greece and raid Athens. They are defeated at the Battle of Marathon.

480   Persian fleet defeated by Athenians at the Battle of Salamis.

479   Greeks defeat Persian armies at Plataea. End of Persian invasions.

477   Delian League set up between Athens and other Greek states.

475	Archaic period ends. Classical period begins.	338	Philip defeats Athenian League at Battle of Chaeronea and dominates Greece.
c449	Peace made with Persia. Athens begins to flourish under its new leader, Pericles, and the Parthenon is built.	336	Philip murdered. Alexander becomes King of Macedonia. The Classical Period ends and the Hellenistic Period begins.
431–404	The Peloponnesian War is fought between Athens and Sparta.	334–323	Alexander founds his empire, invading and defeating the Persian Empire.
404	Athens surrenders to Sparta. The Spartan Empire is created but the Spartans have difficulty controlling it.	323	Alexander dies at Babylon and his huge empire is split by his generals. Ptolemy takes Egypt and Seleucus takes Persia.
371	Spartans defeated by Theban general, Epaminondas, at the Battle of Leuktra. Sparta's power is broken for ever.	200	The age of Greek scientific discovery follows, based around Alexandria in Egypt.
356	Philip II becomes King of Macedonia and his son Alexander the Great is born.	100	Rome gains power in Asia as the Greek civilization declines.
350	Philip tries to take over the city-states.	30	Cleopatra, the last ruler of Ptolemy's family, loses her Egyptian kingdom to Rome.

GLOSSARY

abacus frame with rows of sliding beads on wires or in grooves, which is used for counting

agora large open space in the center of a city, used to hold markets

apprentice someone who works for a skilled person in return for being taught that skill

archaeologist person who finds out about the past by studying old buildings and objects

aristocracy country, or part of a country, which is ruled by a small group of its richest and most powerful people

artifact object made by people, often used to describe things made by people in the past

auloi V-shaped Greek musical instrument made of two pipes that were both blown into at once. One was then played with the right hand and one with the left

cavalry soldiers on horseback who fought outside the group of foot soldiers

chiton simple tunic or robe made from two lengths of cloth fastened at the shoulders and belted at the waist

citizen any member of a country, or part of a country, who is allowed to take part in choosing its rulers

cithara ancient Greek wooden, stringed musical instrument

city-state part of a country that includes the city at its center and the country area around it. Each city-state had its own ruler

civilization to live according to a series of rules and laws. Civilizations are made up of people who live together and obey the same rules.

colony group of people who settle away from their own country, but still consider themselves to be part of it

democracy, demokratia country or part of a country that is ruled by a group of people chosen by all its citizens

dowry money or gifts given by a bride's father to a bridegroom

drachma handful or bundle of obeloi

excavate to dig up buried objects, carefully, to find information about the past

himation type of shawl, worn by Greeks, often over a tunic. The himation was usually made of wool

hoplite ordinary foot soldier in the Greek army

jester person whose job is to amuse people, especially in the home of a rich family

league group of people or countries who share the same beliefs and have the same aims

lyre simple stringed musical instrument, like a small harp

merchant ship ship used by merchants and traders to carry goods to be bought and sold

mosaic design or picture made of small pieces of stone, glass, or clay

myth legend or story that is based on fantasy rather than the truth

obelos thin rod of iron, used as a token, in the same way as money

obol silver coin of ancient Greece

oligarchy country, or part of a country, that is governed by only a few of its people

oracle place where people could consult the gods, usually through a special priest or priestess who might also be known as the oracle

orchestra central area of a Greek **theater** in which most of the play takes place

palaistra school for wrestling, where boys went when they were 14

pedagogue slave who took a Greek child to school

phalanx formation in which the **hoplites,** or foot soldiers, fought in battle

philosopher someone who seeks the truth, a thinker

Renaissance new beginning. A period during the 14th century when people emerged from the Dark Ages and began to study the art and thinking of Classical Greece

Satyr play play involving actors dressed as satyrs, wild men with horses' ears and tails

shrine a place, or object, that is considered important enough to be worshipped. A shrine is often inside a temple

skene back part of the stage in a Greek theater, where actors came on and off, behind which there were dressing rooms

stoa covered area around the outside of a market place

stylus sharpened stick that was used for writing on wax tablets

symposium a drinking party and talk held after a feast. Symposia were often accompanied by musical entertainment

tenant farmer farmer who does not own the land he works. He may rent it or be employed by the owner

trireme Greek warship with sails and three rows of oars, one above the other

tyrant person who ruled a Greek city-state by seizing power

For Further Research

You can find out more about the Ancient Greeks in books and on the Internet. Use a search engine such as www.yahooligans.com to search for information. A search for the word "Ancient Greece" will bring back lots of results, but it may be difficult to find the information you want. Try refining your search to look for some of the people and ideas mentioned in this book, such as "Spartan warriors" or "Greeks gods."

More Books to Read

Pearson, Anne. *Ancient Greece*. New York, DK Publishing, 2003.

Weber, Belinda. *The Best Book of Ancient Greece*. Boston: Kingfisher, 2005.

INDEX